OXYGEN

poetry

by

Cheril N. Clarke

Dedication

For:

The muse and genesis of this collection,

The soul who unearthed it after I'd unwittingly buried it,

and

The love whose openness is allowing me to let it fly free.

Thank you.

Table of Contents

Oxygen is a multi-media poetry project that includes illustrations, video, and audio. Poems that have a spoken word companion have a QR code printed after them to make listening as easy as scanning the page with your smartphone.

Visit the following link to watch a short video of Cheril explaining the inspiration for this title:
https://www.youtube.com/watch?v=ZLFTpnFZBwo&t

Future Memories

When you have memories of me
I hope you smile at the safety you felt
Dance at the freedom you experienced
Sing as you relive the passion, and promises fulfilled
Desires delivered beyond your wildest imagination
I hope you bask in what it felt like to be
Whoever you wanted to be
While you were with me.

Awakening

My chest cracked open like a fault line
Slowly opening us to expose the earth...my core
So vivid
My spirit twisted
Wriggled
Pushed and persisted
Clamoring to break through to the surface
And in seconds I felt it
A BURST!
Of orange and red
I felt the colors emerge from the core of my soul
And then I saw them
Beaming from me like sun rays spraying into the ether
Showering the room with ripples of daybreak hues
My heart exposed itself eagerly
Nakedly
Desperately needing to be accepted as-is
What is this?
Internal bleeding or a life-force healing
I wondered how the experience could be so familiar yet
foreign
I wondered fervently
As a wave of energy
A tide of an epiphany
Twined invisibly
Wrapped around me to infinity
I was cocooned in the moment

No longer my own opponent
I owned it
Them
Her
Us
Me
I levitated
And in suspension I suspended judgement
Of myself
I released guilt
From myself
I felt forces rise from the depths of me to the surface
Splashing over me from the epicenter of my existence
I was covered in myself
A hot sense of awareness of who I am
Who I've always been
Who I'll always be
But whom I'd lost in the process of living
I was back
This awakening was an eruption that would repeat a time or
two before calming
And then there were rumbles throughout the days...weeks
Of how it all came to be
It was erotic
It was hypnotic
It was tantric
It was the abandoning of a dichotomy
Of two lives
Two me's
Too many but still not enough
Because one split into two

OXYGEN

Can never equal a whole
Only two broken parts
I am who I am
I must be one
I've come back to myself
And after the shockwaves, there was peace.
One piece
Me
Whole
Anew
Awakened
Ready to fly.

Scan the QR code below to listen to the spoken word version of this poem. You can also listen by visiting the following link:

https://soundcloud.com/user-677135731

Celebration

Her smile washed over me
Like a million pieces of gold confetti
In slow motion
At daybreak
In an open field
She shimmered
And glowed with possibilities.

She was rhythm
A beautiful progression
Like the gentle tremble of a brush caressing a cymbal
But not the blues, no.

She was a subtle divinity
Her hue a supple oasis
Her voice, a sweet dark tea on a summer's day
Brewed in the depths of her orchard soul
To quench the thirst of only those who are worthy to quaff it
all.

Scan the QR code below to listen to the spoken word version of this poem. You can also listen by visiting the following link:

https://soundcloud.com/user-677135731

Craving

I want it honest
I want it deep

      I want it strong
      I want it long

   And wet

I want it hard
And thick

   Wide
      Pulsing
         Thrusting
            I want it all

I need it now.

    .

   . . .

   .

   .

     I need it....

At Ease

Lose control and step out of the trenches
Abandon your responsibilities
And give in to your darkest needs
Your desires don't have to make sense
The fact that you want what you want is all that matters.

Stand at ease, Soldier.

Relax and explore
The depths and shores of me
Traverse and conquer
Or be conquered, if that's what you crave.

Walk the edge with bare feet
Absorb and devour
Drift in and dissipate
Wade into my waters
I dare you
Make ripples
Make waves
Submerge until you need gills to breathe.

Eternal Love

She wore a brown hat with the brim pulled low
Café au lait skin and eyes that glimmered and shone
With such certainty
That I had to know
Who was she?
     Who was she?
          Who. Was. She?

From across the room
I was hypnotized by her smile
Dimpled and broad. Bright and beckoning.
She was a goddess
In the flesh
And I had to know her
Because the truth is
From the moment I laid eyes on her
I became been transfixed
It was as if
She'd floated in on an ethereal chariot
Distinctly different from all others
Elevated
This woman
Was in a realm of her own
Her energy
An abstruse mystery
Daring me
To step outside of myself
And summon the confidence

To say
Hello
My heart tripped and fumbled over itself as I rose to the
challenge
Taking each nervous step toward her
                Left foot. Right foot.
           Left foot. Right foot.
I walked toward my future
My hands shaking
My head spinning
But
Her casual confidence reeled me into her essence
It pulled me into her beautiful, regal space
That smile
Those eyes
That splendid radiance that was her being
Ordered my steps
And the closer I got
The more I knew
That no matter the risk to my fragile soul or ego
She was worth it
The kind of woman for whom you'd risk it all
And in that moment
That fateful moment when she said yes
Yes to my request
Yes to me
A sophisticated explosion of all the world's possibilities
appeared before me.

Ever since

Life has been a constant unfolding of the very best me—of
we
To be
The very best that we can be
She is my best friend
My soul mate
My teacher
My student
My air and water
She is
My eternal love.

An LP for Us

Like the crackle of a needle hitting a 45"
Our moments together feel
Nostalgic
Even though
They're happening in the present
Something about you feels familiar
Yet new
It's pleasant and exhilarating
In the moment....

I feel a slight static
When your skin touches mine
My body feels more alive than it's been in years
Your touch is sustenance
For a quieted part of a starving soul
A part of me that had been tucked away
Trained to behave
Made to be more
Tame....

But the way your fingertips move so curiously, and eagerly
Traversing my thighs
A flow begins between my legs
Blood rushes to my head
My heartbeat bangs in my chest
That bass
Yes

OXYGEN

My breathing speeds up
To our tempo
I remember what being craved feels like when
I hear you sigh so heavily
Wanting me
And I want you more
Because of how visibly you desire me
Being with you is rest for the weary
Daylight after dreary
Routine

But our days are always short
Hours always feel like minutes
You've got to go
I've got to go
We have to become the past
We already are
Despite crossing paths again
In this life
This is a blip
A crossover that happened

Perhaps
As a rare gift from the universe
But it's not ours to hold onto
We're not meant for forever....

Best that way probably
Even though it hurts
I cling to our memories the way you clung to me
When you made a temporary home inside me

I clutch the reveries that come to me at their own will
The way you gripped my shoulders
And whispered in my ear
Remember me...remember me...I want you to remember me
A song for when you're a long way from
That temporary home
In case you never return
Let our time together live on
In the black waters of our minds
The parts where no one else is allowed
Under the surface
Where they're protected
It was so beautiful to play with you
Goodbye.

Scan the QR code below to listen to the spoken word version of this poem. You can also listen by visiting the following link:

https://soundcloud.com/user-677135731

Anonymous Friend

I need an anonymous friend
One who doesn't know anything about me
Just listens
And shares
But doesn't analyze
Doesn't judge
Doesn't flinch or hurt at what I have to say
Because to each other
We're both anonymous
Just listening
Just living
Just drifting
Just being.

Freedom

Just when I felt the hold on myself loosening up
When I felt my soul relax
And my mind open up
Just enough to chip and dig
Into a heart that's been afraid to express itself
Reality hit me
There is a danger in being so intertwined with another
In sharing and knowing each other so intrinsically well
When your lover is your best friend
And you want to tell your best friend something about your
lover
But you can't
Because they're one
You feel trapped
And in all of these years
You never made another
True friend
Never trusted another person
With access to the passageways to your whole self
Even though
There's nothing inherently wrong with that being
She's private
You're private
You've always been
In a way that still comes off as public
It's been effective as an artist to toe the line of self-expression
and creative license

To let a little trickle out while clinging to the whole
But at some point the entirety gets too big for the vessel
And you need a release
And if you don't let it out
If you don't let it go
It'll find a way on its own
Like ice cream left melting in the sun
It'll run
It might be messy
Because it can't be contained
It needs to breathe.

Journey

She had a smile more radiant than a thousand suns
Hair more beautiful than moonlit fields
Eyes more captivating than the aurora
Skin more fragrant than acres of roses
But with each blink and faraway stare
A word or phrase from her here and there
I knew
There was more
This woman was deep
The kind of woman
Who made the explorer come alive within me
She was an expedition that had to be taken
There was nothing common or basic about her
Multi-layered and kaleidoscopic
Irregularly patterned in a beautifully unique way
For her, I knew I would follow any trace or clue
Dare to take narrow paths anew
I would climb steep hillsides
No matter how slippery or serrated the trail
I had to journey the path where no footsteps left a trace
I had to get to a place in her where no one had the courage or
endurance to go
Through the bushes
Around the bends
Through the ravine
Over the edges
And into the depths

Wherever the maze of her existence led
I would dive to a river's bottom if it meant finding the
broken pieces of her
And getting the opportunity to fuse them back together.

Atop the Banyan Tree

We dined in a Thai sky
Atop the Banyan Tree
Immersed in an enchanting landscape
Above it all
Awake and in tune with each other
So blissful
So divine
Marital bliss captured
Arrested and held
This is the elusive
Desperately sought afterlife
Others search a millennium for
And we've found it
We are so fortunate
To live, learn, love, rest, and rejuvenate in each other
Swaying atop this Banyan Tree
I have never been more sure
You are the woman of my dreams for all of eternity.

Just Words

Always remember
That words
Beautiful
     Loving
          And enchanting
Fall from the same lips
That lie, hurt, and remain closed at times when you need
them the most
Never fall in love with just words.

Drainage

I'm preoccupied with his scent
So strong and alluring
It makes me weak
Vulnerable
Open
Primal
I want to taste its origin.

I'm engrossed in his energy
The way it makes the nape of my neck tingle
When it mingles
With the vim and verve of my being
My nerves stand at attention
We've captured eternity in a moment
And I cling to it
Clutching freedom
In a second
It's heaven
Manna
Nourishment for an abandoned soul.

But then I wash him off me
A priority
The unpleasant part of the ritual
I watch the water
Filled with his residuals
Run down under
Flushed from my system

A cleansing to certify
It's truly over.

Even After I'm Gone

I've been a blessing to many
And a thorn to a few
But what good would I have been
If I didn't say I love you
To all whom I've encountered
During the time that I existed
My thoughts, feelings, and concerns
Have been poured out over thousands of pages
Thus far
Along with all of the intent of my heart
To stand tall and share my God-given talent
No matter how hard
No matter how raw
But to be honest
Even if in a clever way
Through the simple strokes of a pen
Coordinated taps on a laptop
My creativity finally flows freely {{{most of the time}}}
My soul has bled
Everything that I am
I am the black and the white when it all comes down to it
These letters, lines, symbols, and spaces are me
The rhythm and the pauses
The dark and the light
The yin and the yang
The curve and the line
And even after I'm gone
It's in between the lines you'll always be able to find me.

Alyeska

She sat cross-legged on an Alaskan mountaintop
I watched her
Breathing
Becoming
Being
Planted firmly in the swaths of earth that surrounded her
She radiated assuredness and oneness
Absorbent to universal energy
Enhancing her natural power
Commanding life into her body
With clouds at her side
And ocean bottoms a thousand miles beneath her feet
She became a symbol of divinity
An ascension. A breakaway. A force field.
To gaze upon her was to drink in what inner peace – and
inner strength – and deep soul connection looks like.

Feelings

Internal earthquakes
My heart aches
My body shakes
My chest rattles
My eyelashes tremble
Struggling to be the dam against my tears
What happened to my creativity
What happened to my festivity
My constant curiosity and natural proclivities?
How did I lose it all in my newfound stability?

The Edge

When our bodies finally touch
It's like fireworks penetrating a thunderstorm
Light striking in the dark
An explosion in the night
A downpour commences
Bursts of color paint a resurgence of reciprocal seduction
While fire slow dances with rain and
Sea levels rise
Forbidden desires find a place to manifest in plain sight
It's audacious
So addictive….

When your fingertips touch any part of me
My body catapults into a space of unbound passion
Unrivaled stimulation
Limitless imagination
I become undone
And possibilities for a new version of me begin to emerge
You bring me to the edge
On the verge of a place where it's clear the choice is mine
Which way to go
How far to go and
How much sexual power I can unleash on you
Damn, I want to see you.

Love, Pain and Blank Pages

The best art is created from pain
And when you're in a private relationship
With little pain (which is a wonderful thing, but)
You create tensionless work
And when you do experience a low
That pain has nowhere to go
Because
It's private
So you let it sink slowly
Agonizingly
Beneath the sand, rocks and coral
You bury it
Let earthquakes, tsunamis and earth's shifting
Conceal it until it's forgotten.

I've never been the type of writer to let my creations
        collect dust on a desk
Or sit idle on a hard drive
But I am now
If I even create at all
Because the few times I've felt pain
        or anything outside of perfection
Anything deeply personal
I bottled it up
Refused it air
Stifled it to death
Buried it in the black depths of my soul

Drowned it until its lungs bubbled with blood and collapsed
Like a madwoman enraged
In a cage
With nothing or no one to assuage
The guilt
Of being unhappy in the middle of abundance
I ground its lifeless remains to bits
Body-bagged it in brine
All while
Above ground
I walked around with a smile
Living in a divide
The me…and "also me" memes personified
Treading
Barely
Tired
Wearily
I wear this crown
While my feet search for firm ground
I love my hand-crafted life of perfection
But I miss me
The me that was creatively free.
I just want to write what my soul feels
One day
I'll pick up the pieces
Meld them back together, no matter how broken
I'll create wings
And let them fly
Fly high
Above it all
Let them bathe in fresh air

Let them breathe
Let them be reborn in a life anew.
One day.

CHERIL N. CLARKE

Riptide

She came into my life as innocently as a love note
Found on a shore at dawn
A time and space unto herself
She was unexpected but welcomed
Layered and intriguing
Wrapped in pure freedom
In a world where most freeze and
Are unsure
And
Uneasy
She breezes through
Carefree
Airy.

Her touch is divine
Making me uneasy yet relaxed at the same time
Like
Being on the edge of freefalling into bliss
But unable to let go
Restraint overpowers my eagerness
And my desire crawls inward
Where it's safe....

She's danger.

Or love
In its purest form

OXYGEN

I don't know
She's unknown
The very quintessence of a fantasy
A sex goddess…
Who is phenomenal at her job

So I hold back.

But I want to hold her gaze
While receiving
Lock into it. Unblinking. Unflinching.
To investigate the depths of her
Beyond the shore
Into the waves
Wide and narrow
Deep in the barrel
Where our energy connection
Conjures and whirls
A pool at my womb
That calls her name
And pulls her in
Pulls her in
Pulls her in…
And holds on tightly
While I ride waves in her timeless lair

I want to
Skim my fingertips against her jawline
Let my lips trawl and enjoy all contact
Of her skin
On my skin

From the palms of her hands
To her collar bones
To her lip line
To her spine
To her waistline
And the tip of her nose
To the blue polish on her toes
All over
And over
Again
With no end
I want to enrapture her soul
Kiss, lick, bite and hold
Onto the brief moments I have with her
But they're fleeting
Never coming fast enough
And always ending too soon.

She's a riptide.
Glassy, calm and serene on the surface
But with so
Much
More
Below
I know.

She makes my pulse quicken
My breath stop
My tongue parch
My body shiver
Shudder

And tremble
Trying to handle
My inability to let go
And freefall into bliss
I'm caught inside myself
When I lie back
With my back arched
And my toes curled
And her strokes furl
And glide all over me I wonder…
What in the entire Fuck?

I'm under spell
With no distractions
The bliss is a risk
This woman is ecstasy
In spiritual form
A human body
Overtaken by a deity
And I want to devour her
Flip the scene
Turn the table
Clear the floor
Induce spontaneity
Imbue my own brew
Of magik
But I hold back
Because
She's at work
And I am work
And my time is almost up

Time to slide off the crest
Put my feet on the sand
Amble back to the shore
And get back to reality
She's a riptide.

But I keep going back.

Scan the QR code below to listen to the spoken word version of this poem. You can also listen by visiting the following link:

https://soundcloud.com/user-677135731

For further lines explanation, visit
https://genius.com/Cheril-n-clarke-riptide-annotated

Vise Grip

I swore I would never write another word about her
But after 20 years
She still haunts me
She still slithers into my dreams
Still constricts me in her space
Her blue-eyed venom pierces the dark
Behind my eyelids
When my guard is down
While my sleep is sound
When all I want is rest
She glides in jest
All I want is rest.

Undiscovered Treasure

You used to say you wanted to make love to me one day…
But you cannot make love to a stranger
You never knew me
Never made an attempt to learn me on your own
You saw a wall around parts of me and never scratched the
surface
Never tried to scale it or tear it down
Or look around its corners
You never dug in
Never tried to tunnel underneath
Or discover anything beyond the obvious
Never did you venture even the slightest layer beneath my
skin
You marveled at my body
Were enchanted by my beauty
You played with the gold dust and flecks that were easy to see
And missed the entire treasure buried beneath.

Velvet Submarine

She seems more eager to test the boundaries of my will
Every time we drift into each other
The ultimate giver
She refuses me the opportunity to reciprocate in our
moments together
She's flawless and faultless
Not really
But isn't that what the mind always makes us believe when
new beauty lands in our lives?

She's as delicate as a feather
As sweet as a raindrop in the desert
As intricate as the veins in the rose petals
And as flawed as we all are.

But when she and I are alone I'm encased in a lace capsule
A velvet submarine
We're a tight fit
When she climbs on top of me
We're a bateau
A lifetime away from routine and intimate plateaus
I could indulge in her essence forever
She goes below the surface
Inside to feel my textures
And trails the grades of me rough and soft
From my slightly calloused hands
To my untouched promise land

She digs
Goes beyond my tears
Past my damp exterior
To my flooded interior
She's unafraid of burrowing into the grottos
Up, down and around the intimate boroughs of my being
She pays attention and has reawakened me for my true love
And me
And the world
And I'm grateful.

Santhiya

We lay in giant hammocks under leafy banana trees
Eyes to the sky
Souls open to God
Feeling the Thailand breeze
With the sun kissing our bare feet
Experiencing a slice of heaven
Endless oceans accented by lush mountain peaks
Tasting the pleasures of a strange land
It was delicious
To be away from the chaos and noise of the world we knew
A pleasure indescribable
A serenity immeasurable
To be serenaded by the melody of exotic birds and
Common bees
Strange butterflies that begged to be seen
Quite simply, it was pure bliss.

CHERIL N. CLARKE

She Is Love

4:30 a.m.
Awakened
Before the sun and without a clock
Without a jolt
Alive
Fully rested and refreshed
Fulfilled and ecstatic
A pouring out of myself onto the page
My spirit erupts
Charged up from her touch
Her energy
Has me writing like mad
She is love
Not romantic
Just love
Not conditional
No strings
No attachments
Just love
Period.
I understand now
The fog has cleared now.

Subtle vibrations of her pulse through me
For weeks after she drew me in,
under, and inside myself
She is sacred divinity with wings spread to infinity
She is a cover

OXYGEN

A consecrated space with a splash of earthly crass
(Who said love didn't have a bit of sass?)

Island girl with the flower in her hair
On the right side
With her signals out
She's euphoria.

Our intimacy is palpable and pure
Exploratory and revealing
Below the surface
Pieces of my soul scratch and clamor to get out
Because they've tasted sweet fingertips of freedom
From under the armor
Slices of my spirit claw an opening to breathe
To see
To be exposed
And feel the light
To feel dawn
To dance in the sun
The day has not yet caught up
But I know there is now light at 4:30 a.m.
Because of her
Because she is love
And because
She shared it with me.

CHERIL N. CLARKE

Rest in Me

When you feel yourself growing weary
From the journey to contentedness
Worn out
From the hunt of passion
And fatigued by its elusiveness

When your heart grows weak
From the crush of rejection
Or worse
Aloofness
The repetition
The mundane
The predictable
The banal
Darling, come rest in me.

Touch

I swear
I could write 10,000 words
From the sensation of your touch.

CHERIL N. CLARKE

Water and Stone

People change
Like the jagged edge of mountain rock
Being smoothed down over time
The constant flow of water over stone
From a drizzle to rain that shoots down in sheets
Water
Gentle water
Can wear down an alp
Until it shines like a crystal in the sun
And all showers that follow
Are an endless stream of kisses
To and from the most unlikely lovers.

Paint

He had eyes like the Caribbean Ocean
And I wanted to swim the depth of them
His stare stole my breath
Arrested my eyes
Shook my thighs

It's too bad
He was about as exciting
As watching paint dry
A true reminder
That some people
Should remain passersby.

Liberated

All I want
Is to stand barefoot in the rain
To sing, to dance
To strip from my clothing

I want to lose it all. Everything.
Bra
Panties
Let them tumble to the ground

I want to walk in the sparkling drops from God unjudged by
the thoughts from man
To unearth pleasures that have become entombed in decades
of proper living
I want to be free
I want to be me
I just want to be
Liberated. *

*Previously published in the short story, "The Edge of Bliss,"
by Cheril N. Clarke.

Surrender

The silence that fills the space where your voice used to be
      is deafening
Unsettling
It feels like crash-landing from the highest point of the
universe into an infinity of black
The pain drowns me in darkness
I'm smothered by the audacity of my own selfish actions
Alone in my shame
Me alone to blame
I failed you
I failed myself
And now I sleep on a bed of fire
Asphyxiated by smoke
And soot
And dust
Embers singe my fingertips
My heart is engulfed in an inferno
Surrounded by black roses with withered edges
I can't escape
My soul is scraped, battered, bruised, broken, and shattered
I feel destroyed
Tell me we're stronger than this
Tell me you still love me
I surrender to the consequences of my actions
Tell me I won't drown in flames forever.

Tattooed Mermaid

She's so ladylike
Sometimes
A gentlewoman
Who bends the definitions
Of masculine and feminine
Beautiful androgyny
An ocean child
Frolicking naked
Chiseled and elastic
She wears seashells for earrings
And ink for sleeves.

A rock and sway
A spectrum
A spectacle
She's a current of her own
Many meters below
When she rises at dawn
The waters part
Her red tail and green scales
Ebb and flow
Dancing against on the ocean's floor
As sunlight floods the corridor
The path to her...
Calls me
Pulls me
Draws me from afar
From lifetimes away

OXYGEN

From consciousness
From sleep
I can still hear her
Still feel her salt-water skin
Still taste her candy-coated tongue
And smell her distinct fragrance
But I fight the appeal
Remembering the tears
Remembering the years
When this tattooed mermaid
Sucked the life out of me
I can't float with her and breathe.

Oxygen

She plays the harp strings of my sacral chakra
Under a canopy of trees
Where birds sing
And the smallest factions of life breathe
She explores the lines and curves of my physique freely
And we collapse into a quiet melody
In a private ceremony where she invokes passion
Fosters pleasure
Releases pain
Releases trauma
She heals by erasing guilt and shame
And now I feel myself floating
From the top of a rainforest
Down into a river
Where I'm alone with another me
Who looks at me curiously
Like a reflection of a lost identity
How did I become split into we?

I'm in another reality with truth
And she's looking at me
Wondering why I abandoned her
I begin to speak but halt
The risk of drowning is too much
Too real
So I talk with my eyes
And keep my lips sealed
{{{I'm sorry}}}

This other me dives into my sacral chakra and swims
upstream
My knees hit the river floor
Hands next
On all fours
Dust kicks up around me and
I try to push off the ground and get back on my feet
But struggle
Too submerged
Seaweed wraps around my feet
Bubbles trickle from my nose
Precious air escapes me
I'm stuck at the bottom and see her look at me once more
The other me
With a mix of pity and forgiveness
The corners of her eyes crinkle
The sign of a suppressed smile
And I start to feel warmth
She's come closer to me
Closer to home
I feel myself rising, singing, "Come back to me"
The wet jungle unshackles my feet
And in the distance, finally, I can see light on the surface
Sunlight dapples from above
Rays spray down desperately needed heat
My blood is rushing
She reminds me she's still there
I feel the warmth of her presence
A tightening and binding
A homecoming inside me

OXYGEN

I accept her as the gift that she is
I promise never to shut her away
Because she's a part of me
And all parts of me are worthy
We break the surface
Burst through its tension with force and intention
And finally, I can breathe again.

Scan the QR code below to listen to a piano and vocal arrangement created from a few lines in this poem. You can also listen by visiting the following link:
https://soundcloud.com/user-677135731

Sweetwater

The way she stares into my eyes
And cups my face
In the palm of her hands
So gentle
So loving
So comforting
I bathe in her love

She is Sweetwater
She is life
She is my past, present, and future
My love
She quenches the thirst of my soul.

Off Currents

You said that I was so special to you
That I had been since the day we met
And as we cycled in and out of each other's lives
Me propelling toward you
You steering away from me
Like confused schools of fish
Around and around
Off-balance
In and out
Uncoordinated and unsynchronized
Sometimes I believed you
On the days we went upstream together
But I knew
Deep down
It wasn't true
We were off currents
Splitting from each other one moment
And violently crashing into one another the next
Unhealthily
I've long stopped trusting my ears before my eyes
Words are just words without indication of actions taken to
back them
It is possible you actually believed yourself
But truly, I was too much for you.

Underwater

Love and life ensnare me
Weighing me down like anchors
Refusing to let "I feel great" last for longer than a few days
I'm either walking on the ocean
Or being dragged underwater
These two L's giveth and taketh away
Salvation and disaster
Fraternal twins
With a wicked sense of humor
They ensure
My stay on earth will be a constant loop of wishing, working,
obtaining, being ungrateful for;
Of feeling guilty about, feeling misunderstood, and then back
to wishing
It's no wonder
I constantly feel underwater.

White Lies

I can hear them in your voice
In the split second when you pause to edit what you were
going to say
To what you think I want to hear

I can pluck them from your saccharine lines like rotten fruit
from a vine
Tossing them aside
But not without making a note
That nothing you say should be taken too seriously
Never taken too deeply
Because sprinkled through it all
Are always little white lies
I can see it in your eyes.

Love's Rebirth

I knew the moment I saw her
That I'd taken the last step I needed to.

After ten thousand strides in the wrong direction
Just to turn around and go
Again, in the wrong direction
Month after month
Year after year
Decade after lonely decade
With eyes that were quickly becoming dead from the fatigue
of it all
The quest for love
The quest for intimacy
The quest for touch
The search for honesty
An endless expedition of futility, it seemed
Until I saw her
Beyond the clouds
In the seven-hued arch
I stopped and stared
Reeled in by the soul I'd been searching for
My eyes were reborn bright and alive
My worn face and exhausted soul sprang anew.

Wildfire

One second at a time
You let the heat grow
One moment at a time
You let the embers catch
Days, weeks, months
You let me catch, grow, blaze and become a roaring fire
My body, my mind, my spirit burned....

Why did it take you so many years
To tend to my desires
Why was I not enough
Why did it take my hunger for touch screaming into the
streets to capture your attention
When you were next to me the whole time
My desperation became a flame
Wild and enraged
A giant flare that blazed for the attention of someone to put
it out
I wanted it to be you.

Groundswell

To catch a glimpse of her
Is to witness a natural wonder
Morning glory
Magical splendor
The most remote, forgotten, yet desperately needed rendition
of humanity
She is sacred magnetism
With intentional touch
An élan of a wave traveling across the ocean
Peeling back layers of reluctance
Of hesitation
Of fear
To allow full expression of self
For those who have been called and reeled into her realm
Into her ecstatic flow
She knows what she exudes
And comforts whom she attracts
She is groundswell of loving energy.

CHERIL N. CLARKE

Safer in My Head

I don't know how many times I have to learn
To be quiet
To say less
To share little
To be more invisible
You can't get hurt if you go unseen
You can't get attacked if you go unheard
I need to train myself to
Lay low
Beneath the horizon
To become a barely-felt breeze in the atmosphere....

I wonder what it's like
To be a single tree in a land of forests
Or a single leaf on that single tree
Quiet
Unnoticed
But unscathed.

I'm safer in my head
Where my characters are friends
And
I can bare it all
Share it all
Play with it all
Live with it all
And die with it all

In my cocoon of creativity
Maybe
If only my art affected only me when released…but it
doesn't.

I'm safer in my head.

CHERIL N. CLARKE

Gagged, Bound and Blindfolded

Constantly living outside yourself
In the rules of society
In the circles of social acceptance
Unwilling to just be
And explore
And dig
Unearth
Discover
Know
Embrace
Love
Hate
Endure
Understand
Embrace
All parts of yourself
Is to live gagged, bound, and blindfolded.
Don't.
Live freely
Live uniquely
Live authentically
Break free
Shake free
Force yourself to see
The dark and the light
The beautiful and the ugly
The brightness and shadows.
Taste the bitter and the sweet of your existence

OXYGEN

Live freely
Live uniquely
Live authentically
Break free and be.

Mirror Image

You are angelic indemnity
From negative thoughts and natural negativity
You stand with and cover me
Magnifying my talents
My blessings
My fortunes
My gifts.

In front of my eyes
You purify the sea that embodies me
Desalinating and decontaminating
When tears flow
And energy releases.
My life force rushes and courses unadulterated internally
And I begin personifying what you saw and see
Externally.

We become one.

Undertow

The allure of his cologne
Of his spontaneous lifestyle
Of his willingness to adore and worship me
Pulls me under

The strength of his arms and back
As they lift and hold me up against a wall
And explores,
Pulls me down further

Where only open-mouthed exhalations keep me alive
And though he keeps pulling me under
I bathe in his outlandish passion for me
He's the one
The oxygen mask that I've needed.

The Most Beautiful City in the World

It's magnificent
The old world charm of cobblestone streets
And horse-drawn carriages
Morning pastries
And late night river strolls
Montreal is the perfect blend of old and new
Of the future promises
And past treasures
Of incredibly beautiful men and women
Friendly French
A true pleasure indeed
It is the most beautiful city in the world
A lover I will never forget
A destination of which I will always dream
Full of joyous memories.

One Hour with You

It's all I need to feel revitalized
Empowered
And ready to live to my fullest potential

Une heure avec toi

C'est tout ce qu'il me faut pour me sentir revitalisé
Habilité
Et prête à vivre à mon plein potentiel.

Sad Love Song

The sound of your footsteps
On the way out
Drowns me for all of eternity.

Awash in Vulnerability

The moment I step into her sphere
The struggle begins
Serenity vs. anxiety
Time running out vs. time not existing at all

The instant her stare meets mine
My breath staggers
My lips quaver
And my fingertips search for something
Anything
To grab onto
To steady myself for the impending ride
The inevitable jaunt into a dazzling space
Where I forget everything
Where a graze sends ripples of shock and enchantment
From the crown of my head to the tips of my toes
And I am awash in vulnerability.

Bi-lines

It's the arch and strength in her shoulders
The roundness and depth of her eyes
The relentlessly enchanting energy that surrounds her
That has me transfixed.

Meanwhile
It's the daring way he moves through life
The adventurer, the explorer, the fun lover that encapsulates
him
That keeps me so drawn.

Her protective instinct and formidable loyalty
His spontaneity and reckless behavior
Her commitment and bottomless capacity
For love
For nurturing
For understanding
For teaching, guiding, mastering and leading that have me
floating on streams of eternal gratitude.

Searching for Ecstasy

It's here
I know it is
Joy
Wonder
Intrigue
Shock and surprise
Never-ending delight
The stuff of childhood years
Before school and societal adaptation snuffed it out of us
For the rest of my days I'm on a mission
Searching for ecstasy
Clutching even tiny slivers if it crosses my way
And I'll create it as a way of life through continuous seeking,
loving and learning.

Bronze-Skinned Goddess

She is a bronze-skinned goddess
I spend my days fantasizing about.
She floats into my dreams
Infiltrates my streams of consciousness
Without warning.

When I'm lost at sea
She is a blazing bonfire at night
Sending smoke signals
Thousands of miles to and from the shore.

I swim to her fervently
Assuredly
Expecting ecstasy and exuberance
Upon experiencing her touch
But Love
My love
Is ever elusive
A figment of my imagination
I spend an eternity trying to reach.

CHERIL N. CLARKE

If you enjoyed the book, please consider leaving a review on Amazon.com.

Please also consider posting a photo of you holding the book to your favorite social media account and tagging @Cherilnc on Twitter, @CherilNClarke on Facebook, or @cheril.n.clarke on Instagram.

For more work by Cheril N. Clarke please visit cherilnclarke.com.

www.ingramcontent.com/pod-product-compliance
Lightning Source LLC
Chambersburg PA
CBHW060135050426
42448CB00010B/2129